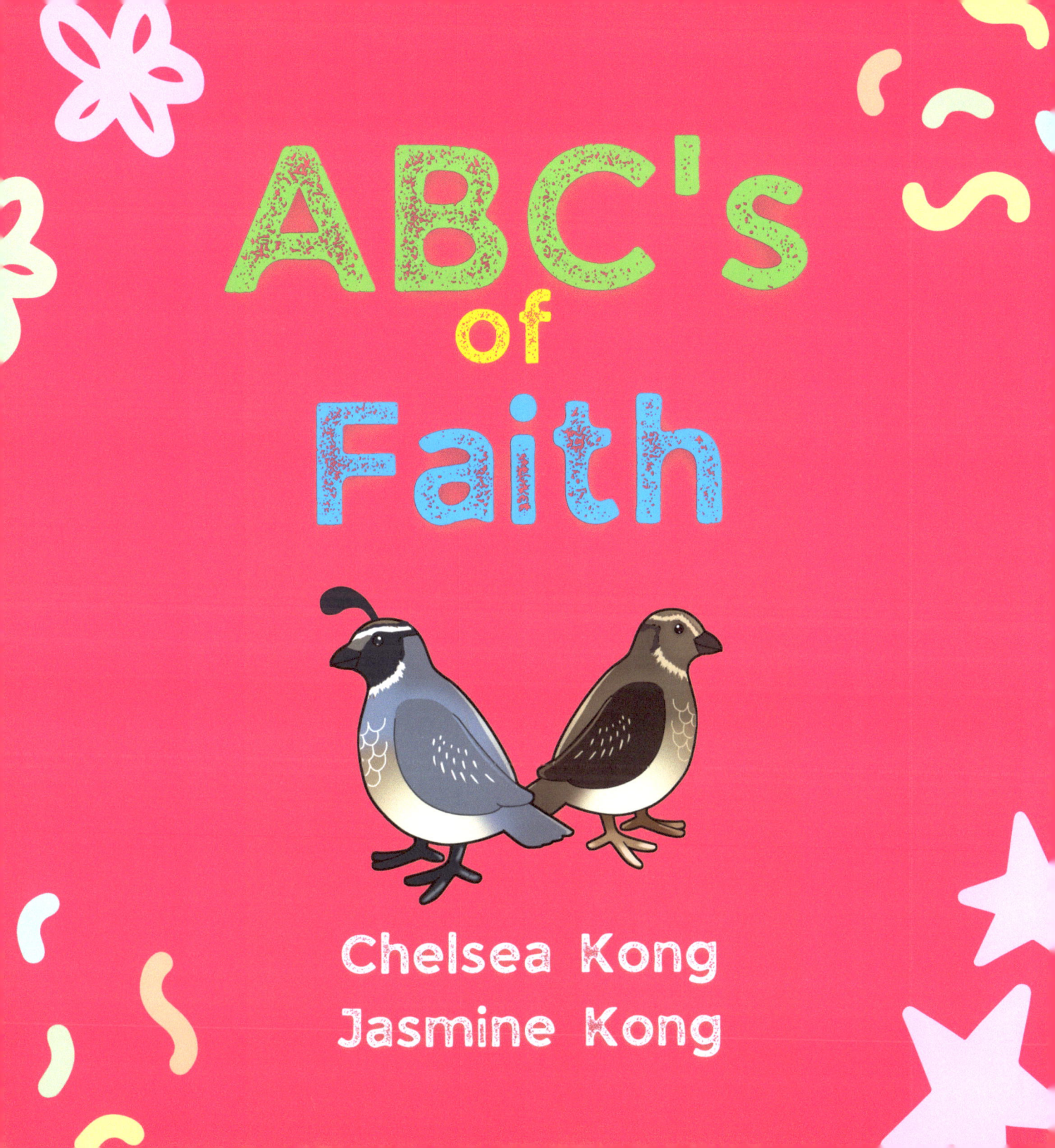

© 2023-2024 Chelsea Kong

All rights reserved. All images used in this book are licensed copies from their respectful owners including myself, Jasmine, Canva, and Freepik. This book or any portion thereof may not be reproduced or used in any manner whatsoever without the express written permission of the publisher except for the use of brief quotations in a book review.

Printed in 2023-2024, Made in Toronto, Canada
ISBN: 978-1-990399-21-3
Library and Archives Canada

A

Apple

Adam and Eve ate apples.
One of many fruits that God made.

B

Bread

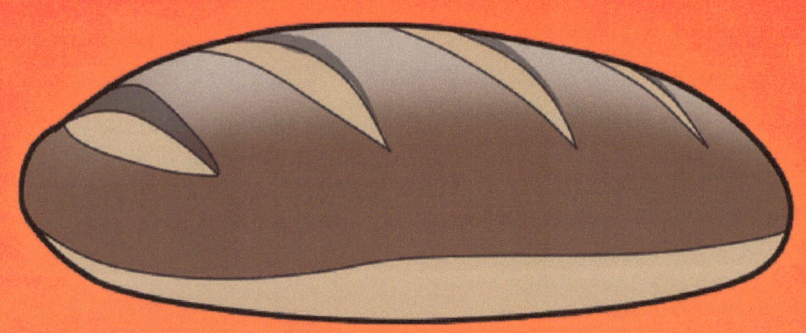

Jesus broke bread, gave thanks, and gave it to His disciples and the 5000.

C

Candles

Candles are placed on candlesticks to give light to lamps, temples and all in the house.

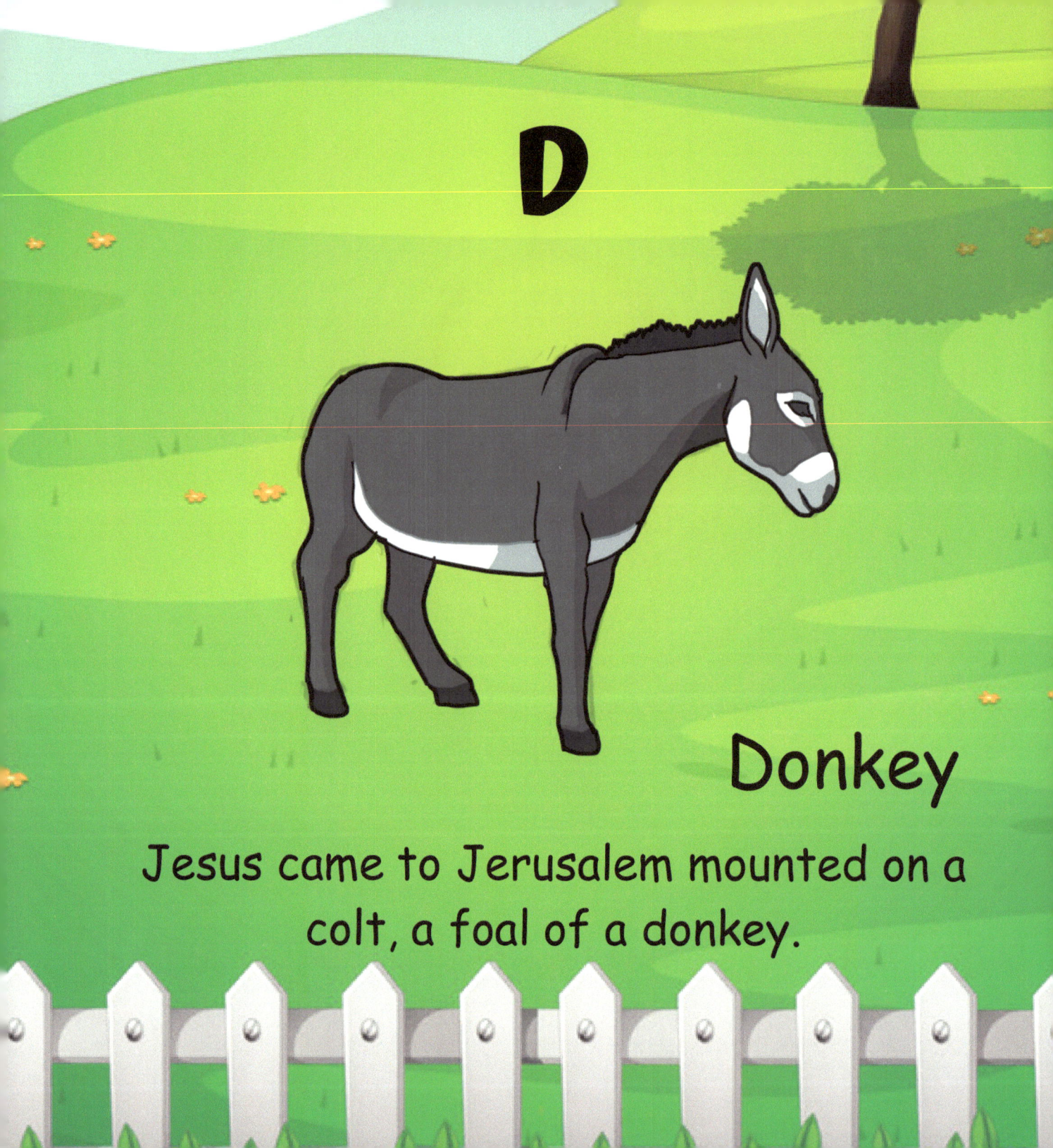

E

Eagle

God will lift us up on wings like eagles.
We will go high and see far.

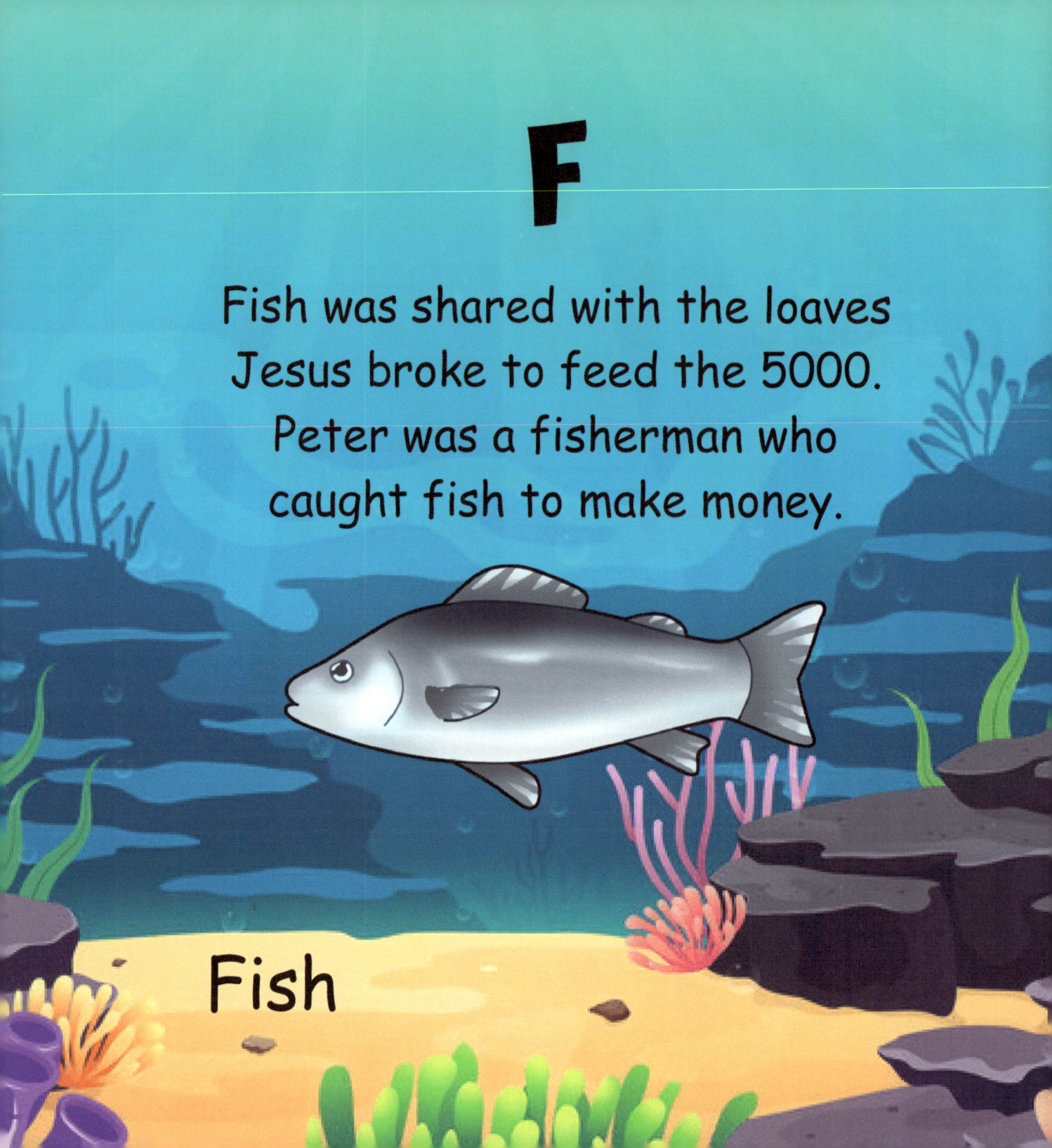

F

Fish was shared with the loaves Jesus broke to feed the 5000. Peter was a fisherman who caught fish to make money.

Fish

G

Gold

Gold is used for palaces, temples, treasures and things for the home.

H

Harp

People and angels use harps
to play songs, hymns, and praises.

I

Israel

The land God has promised to Abraham and his children and their families. God gave Jacob the name Israel.

J

Jesus

Son of God who was sent to save the world. He lives forever in heaven.

K

Key

Keys open doors, chests and
keep special and secret things safe.

L

Linen

Linen is used for priest's clothes and worn by Jesus after He was laid to rest.

M

Myrrh

One of the Magi gave myrrh
to Jesus as a gift.
Esther used myrrh to look more
beautiful before seeing the King.

N
Nuts

God gave nuts and seeds
to Adam and Eve as food.
It is also healthy to eat.

O
Olives

Olives can be found in trees and are used as oil for baptism, lamps and food.

P

Pig

Jews call pigs unclean.
Evil spirits made pigs run away from Jesus.

One evening, the quail came to the desert, and the camp became full of them. God gave quail to the Jews as food.

R

Ram's horn

Ram's horns made Jericho's wall fall.
Priests blow on the Feast of Trumpets.

S

Sword

Swords are used for fighting and guarding. God gave swords to the angels to fight against evil and His Word is our Sword.

T

Tent

Jews used tents in the desert to sleep.
God's Tabernacle is used for meeting God.

U
Utensils

Bowls, jars, and pots are utensils used in homes and temples.

V
Vegetables

On the third day, God made plants. Daniel ate only vegetables and was just as healthy as those who ate meat.

W

Wood

Wood is used for cooking,
altars and ornaments.
It is burned in a fire to keep people warm.

y
Yarn

Blue, purple, and scarlet yarn was used for the Tabernacle curtains and the priest's clothing.

Z Zion

Zion the City of David.
The mountain and church of God.

SALVATION PRAYER

God, I know I sinned against you. Forgive me for the wrong that I have done. I believe that Jesus Christ died on the cross for me. That He rose from the grave so that after three days. I can have His long-lasting life. Come into my heart to be my Lord and Savior. I choose to turn away from my sins and I choose to follow you. Lead me to walk with you. Keep me safe and teach me your ways. Stop every bad thing in my life that has an open door to hurt me. Close those doors. Holy Spirit fill me now in Jesus' name. Amen.

BAPTISM IN THE HOLY SPIRIT

Jesus, you are the one that fills me with Your Spirit. Come, Holy Spirit, and come into my life and fill me to be so full of Your presence. Come with your fire too. Thank you for the gift of tongues in Jesus' name. Amen.

Open your mouth and let the words come out that God gives you. It will be words that you don't know what they mean. You can ask God what it means. You need to let Him talk through you every day to grow this gift.

He will bring you closer to God and you will know Jesus more. You will have power from God to do great things and know things.

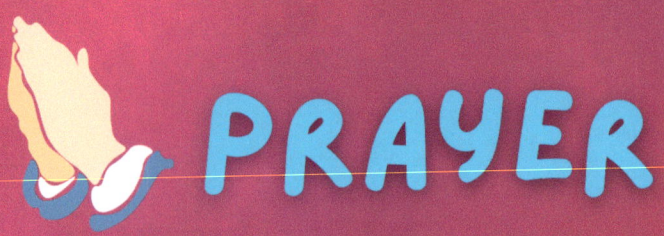

PRAYER

Thank you, God for ABCs. Thank you for teaching me words and some names in the Bible. Teach me more about ABCs and how to use it every day in Jesus' name. Amen.

Message from the Author

This book teaches the basics of each letter of the alphabet based on words from the Bible. There is also another ABC book that teaches about people in the Bible called ABC for People in the Bible. It will be great for children to learn from this book, too. It will get them excited and interested in reading the Bible. It is good to teach them early. Give your children a chance to learn early while they are still young. Then they will not leave the faith even when they grow old. Make it fun for them to learn the word of God!

OTHER PRODUCTS

- Knowing God
- How to Hear God's Voice
- New Life in Jesus
- Loving Israel
- God's Gifts/Spiritual Talents
- Meeting God
- Word Power
- Fruit of the Spirit
- The Tabernacle
- Bride for Jesus
- A Life of Prayer
- Live Free
- Who am I in Jesus
- Walk in Love
- God's Favor
- Man of God
- Woman of God
- How to Use Money
- God's Wisdom
- Fasting
- See Jerusalem and Bethany
- First Fruit Offering
- Feast of Trumpets
- Day of Atonement
- Feast of Tabernacles
- Counting the Omer
- Festival of Lights
- Glory, Presence, and Holy Spirit
- Live in God's Presence
- Pentecost
- See Galilee, Nazareth, and Tiberias
- Hear God Speak
- Knowing Jesus
- Knowing Holy Spirit
- A Healthy Life and Healthy Life Work Book
- Smokey the Cat
- Passover Unleavened Bread
- Resurrection Life
- Proverbs 31 Woman
- Loving Jesus
- The Blessing
- Revival
- Chelsea Learns Hebrew
- Thanksgiving
- Give Thanks
- Jesus Birth

OTHER PRODUCTS

Loving Jesus: Bride and Groom
Proverbs 31 Woman
ABC of People in the Bible
Colours in the Bible
The Seven Spirits of God
Numbers in the Bible
Aglee the Eagle
An Eagle's Life

Devotionals
31 Day Devotional

Inspirational/Other
Chelsea's Psalms and Poems
Your Daily Meal: Chelsea's Photo Album
Chelsea's Psalms and Poems 2

Puzzle Books
Biblical Puzzle Book Vol 1-5
Bible Puzzles for Young Children Book 1-3
Biblical Puzzle for Children Books 1-5

Teaching Series
How to Hear God's Voice Teaching Guide & Audio Book
Relationship with God, Jesus, Holy Spirit Guide
Knowing God, Jesus, Holy Spirit Guide & Audio Book
Flowing in the Prophetic

Teaching (Non-Sale on my website)
Purim
Passover
Resurrection

More books to come!

BOOK REVIEWS

More books on Amazon, Kobo, and Barnes and Noble, Smashwords, and IngramSpark.
https://chelseak532002550.wordpress.com/

More books on Amazon, Kobo, and Barnes and Noble, Smashwords, and IngramSpark.
https://www.amazon.com/author/chelseakong

Please leave a review and share with friends to help the author continue to write more books to reach more readers. Thank you so much for your support.

Review!

About
CHELSEA KONG

She is a writer, creative arts and digital media artist, skilled administration and certified PCP (Payroll Compliance Professional), and podcaster. Chelsea also served in a variety of roles, from audiovisual, photography, to assisting on the worship team, and ministry team. She also has a passion for families being united.

Chelsea has been a guest on Unity Live Radio, The Lady Tracey Show, and How to Live for Christ and is highly recommended by a Proud Christian blog. She is also a guest blogger. A few of her books have been featured in YourAuthorHub, etc. She graduated from Hotel and Restaurant Management, Digital Media Arts, Office Administration, Payroll Compliance Professional, and experience working with children. Chelsea lives in Toronto, Canada. She mainly writes children's books, stories, bridal writing, poems, lyrics for songs, words of encouragement, blessings, prayers, and jokes. The author of How to Hear the Voice of God, the Bridal Collection, Knowing God, etc. She also has her own Bible Puzzle books and other inspired products. Her podcast channel is called Chelsea K on Anchor, Spotify, and iTunes.

Please check my website to find out more:
https://chelseak532002550.wordpress.com/

About
JASMINE KONG

She is a self-employed artist in graphics, web, and gaming. She graduated from Tradigital Animation and has studied Graphic Design. She produces her own graphics for commissions. Her graphics range from simple to more complicated. Her favourite art style is anime and she enjoys watching Japanese anime. She also produces graphics suitable for websites. She has also been featured in an anime book and won first prize for the contest. Everyone who knows about her artwork enjoys it. She has even had an opportunity to show students how to do a bit of origami.

www.ingramcontent.com/pod-product-compliance
Lightning Source LLC
Chambersburg PA
CBHW041414010526
44107CB00016B/1165